Witold Lutoslawski

THREE CHILDREN'S SONGS

**for three equal voices
(SSA)**

**Based on words by
L. KRZEMIENIECKA and A. BARTO**

**Edited by
MARIE POOLER**

CHESTER MUSIC

Three Children's Songs
A Night in May
S.S.A.

Based on Words by
L. Krzemieniecka

Witold Lutoslawski
Edited by Marie Pooler

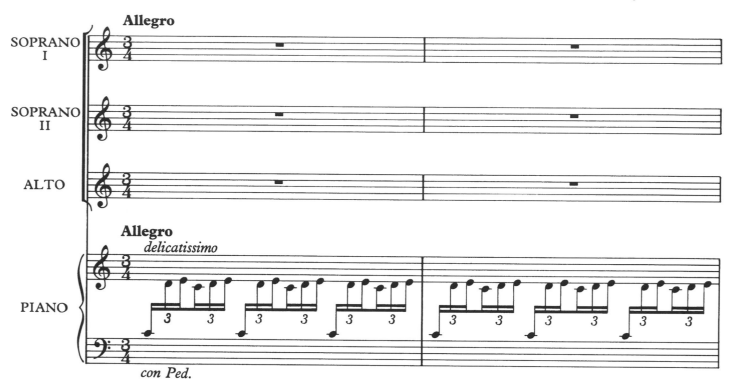

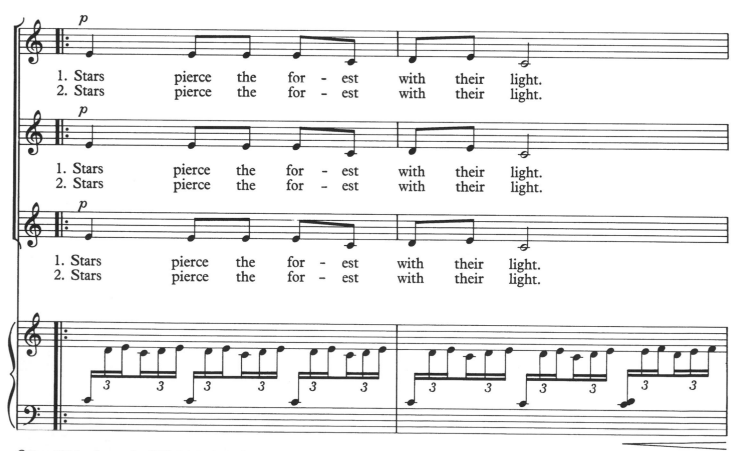

1. Stars pierce the for - est with their light.
2. Stars pierce the for - est with their light.

1. Stars pierce the for - est with their light.
2. Stars pierce the for - est with their light.

1. Stars pierce the for - est with their light.
2. Stars pierce the for - est with their light.

CH 55119

Come, share with us this sil - ver night.
Come, share with us this sil - ver night.

Come, share with us this sil - ver night.
Come, share with us this sil - ver night.

Come, share with us this sil - ver night.
Come, share with us this sil - ver night.

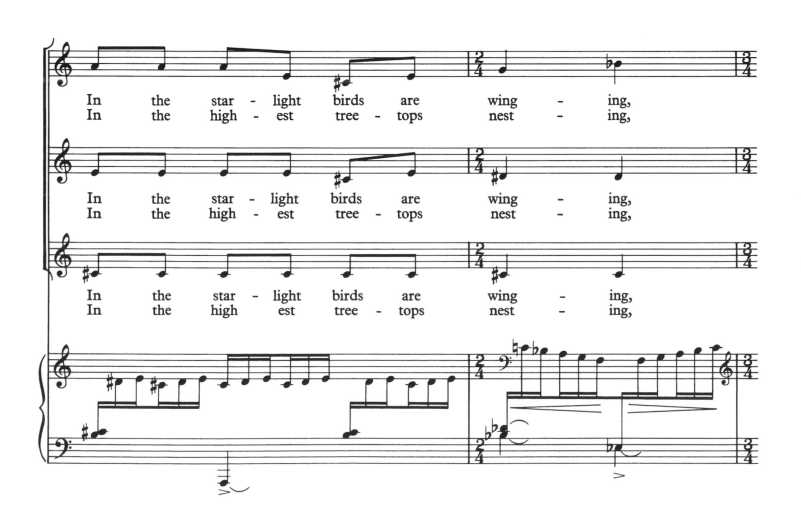

In the star - light birds are wing - ing,
In the high - est tree - tops nest - ing,

In the star - light birds are wing - ing,
In the high - est tree - tops nest - ing,

In the star - light birds are wing - ing,
In the high est tree - tops nest - ing,

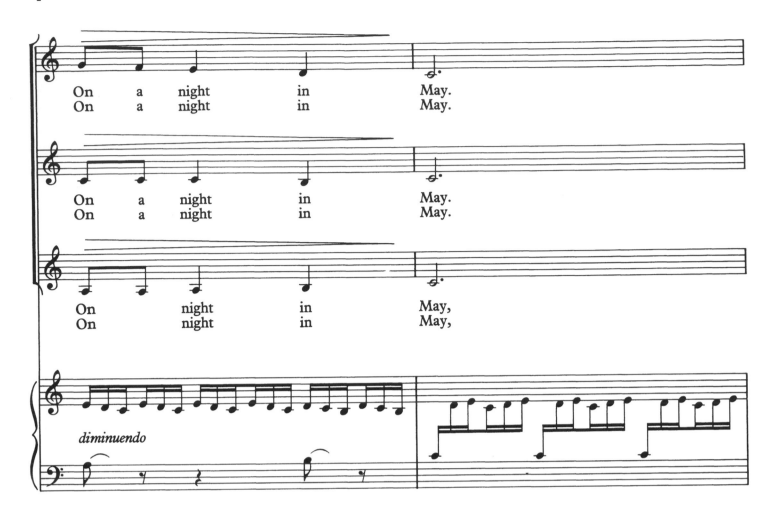

On a night in May.
On a night in May.

On a night in May.
On a night in May.

On night in May,
On night in May,

diminuendo

pp

poco rit.

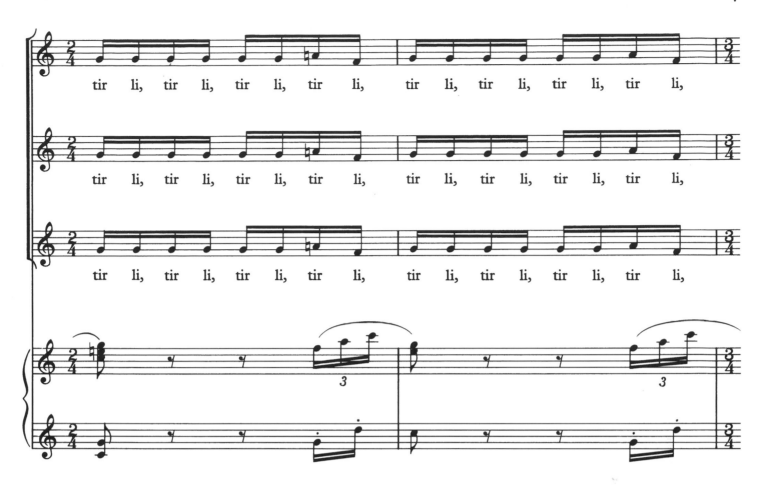

tir li, tir li, tir li, tir li, tir li, tir li, tir li, tir li,

tir li, tir li, tir li, tir li, tir li, tir li, tir li, tir li,

tir li, tir li, tir li, tir li, tir li, tir li, tir li, tir li,

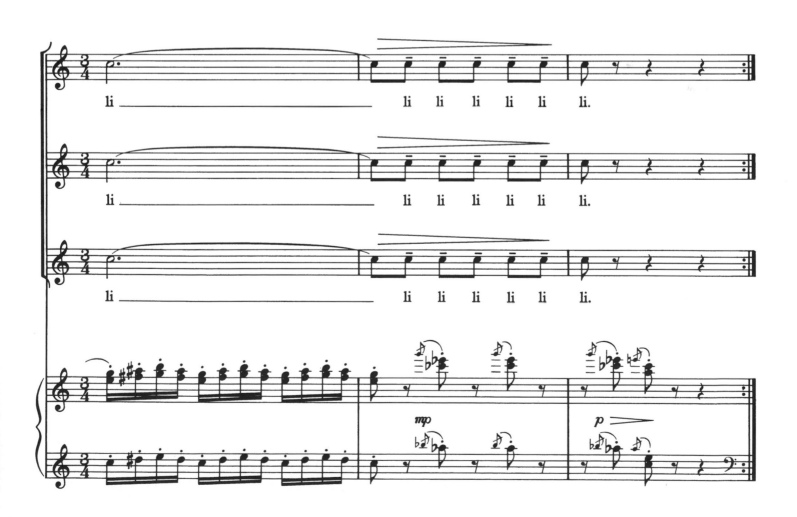

li _____ li li li li li li.

li _____ li li li li li.

li _____ li li li li li li.

Windowpanes of Ice
S.S.A.

Based on Words by
A. Barto

Witold Lutoslawski
Arranged by Marie Pooler

In Every Seashell
S.S.A.

Based on Words by
A. Barto

Witold Lutoslawski
Arranged by Marie Pooler